POEMS OF
LOVE AND DEATH

Books by George MacBeth

George MacBeth

POEMS OF
LOVE AND DEATH

ATHENEUM

New York

1980

Some of these poems have appeared in: *Ambit, The American Poetry Review, The Bennington Review, Encounter, The London Magazine, Men Only, The New Review, The New Statesman, The PEN Broadsheet, Poetry Dimension, The Scotsman, Stand,* and *The Times Literary Supplement.* One has been published as a Sceptre Press pamphlet, and one has appeared in a Sceptre Press anthology. To the editors of these magazines and anthologies, and to the Sceptre Press, my acknowledgements are due.

Contents

POEMS OF
LOVE AND DEATH

FOR

Lisa St. Aubin de Teran

By Way of a Prologue

I

Imagine, in England,
Someone who is looking at the sun moving
Through the dilapidated remnants
Of the Eastern hemisphere. His name is Harry, but
He is not, or is not yet,
That insouciant, military progenitor
Whom all will recall
From the history of Agincourt. He is Harry Crosby.

II

Imagine, gentlemen,
That he has a pair of binoculars
Constructed of good German glass
And that he is watching that red, singular orb
With a kind of passion
Most of us give only to women. He is utterly possessed
With the magnificent, celestial
Burnish of the solar energy. He is Harry Crosby.

III

Imagine, in your mind's eye,
Two people lying dead on a bed in
A small ninth-floor room
In an uptown hotel in New York City. It is nineteen
Twenty nine
And the stock market is about to crash, but
That is not why the young man
With the smoking gun in his hand has fired. He is Harry Crosby.

IV

Imagine the winter sun
Glittering through the forgotten window on the still
Beautiful eyes
Of the girl he has killed by a shot in the brain

3

      Or who has perhaps
    Killed herself, we are not sure, by a shot
      Pre-arranged with him, or
Not pre-arranged, and has left him alive. He is Harry Crosby.

V

      Imagine that just one second
    Ago the blood welled from a single wound in her head
      And the girl died
In the path of the sun driving across Manhattan
      Towards a new decade
    And imagine that Harry Crosby who has been
      In love with her, as with many others,
Has taken the last light on his shaking brow. And the play is
      about to begin.

V I

      Imagine that somewhere in Heaven
    The nationality of catastrophe has become incidental
      And that Harry Crosby
Is a myth of England. Yes, it seems different now,
      I know, to be imagining
    Someone so close to home on that lonely bed
      In the winter light
With a head wound. With a terrible sickness of the heart.

V I I

      Imagine, perhaps, though,
    That the sickness for which this improbable hero died
      Was a little thing
No larger than the tiny crozier in a woman's forks
      For which the sun stooped
    Out of the black sky, and sold his name.
      Imagine that Harry Crosby
Lifted his heart, and the sun took it. And he was you.

The Death of Iris Bodmer
1909–1978

When I saw the QE 2 edge
    Downstream in the Hudson River
At twilight, I didn't know that
    Iris Bodmer was aboard in

Cabin 4207. Nor did I know,
    Or anybody, so far as one can tell,
That Iris Bodmer would step into the ocean
    Off Honolulu, and drown. She was too rich

To live. Or too full of abject memories
    Of the gay twenties. Or simply too
Old. But she has been swiftly translated
    Into the grey substance of water, the

Green substance of myth. For me.
    At least for me. And why this
Has not happened, or not yet happened,
    To those other, closer few

Who retired during my absence into
    The off-shore or mid-ocean
Separateness of what has been sometimes called
    Their deaths, I can hardly say.

I mean Alan, and Martin. I mean
    Guy, too, and Uncle Max, not
To forget those unhuman but perhaps equally
    Momentous beings departed. It seems

More tragic than poignant how
The imagination qualifies our
Precise griefs into blank walls, or delayed
Follies, yet offers a flourish

To puff the unremarkable niggle
Of oddity one can feel about
Such a stranger as Iris Bodmer. And how
She died. It seems a distressing

Irrelevance. And yet, it may be,
That romantic leap into the
Sundering ocean annihilated something proper
To remember as how

My own father survived, uplifted,
And yet a little damaged, by
That suave decade of the 1920s he and
Iris Bodmer both came from. It may

Be such nicer connections that make
The words flow now. And the chance
To say, after all, some elegy for those two
Original poets, nourished

On white light, like genius, and
For those two helpless beasts, with
Their fur and their mute eyes, textured
With the solvent beauty of love.

Thank you, Iris Bodmer. May you sleep
Sound and quiet in the bed
Of the long Pacific. And may my friends join
From their graves in the grief of your poem.

The Burmese Cats

I

Once we went out for a walk, in the park, or by the river.

It was a Sunday, or a holiday, I don't quite remember which any more.

Anyway, it was good weather, and we both enjoyed our walk and the weather.

And, as we walked, we came up from the river past a high wall.

I I

And on the wall two beautiful Burmese cats were walking, near an open window.

It was one of those lyrical moments you read about, and sometimes remember later.

The two cats in withering sunlight, and the two of us looking up.

I suppose you could say it was a kind of awakening, or a vision.

I I I

Except that the two Burmese cats were just cats, and we were just us.

Afterwards, we went on with our walk, across the Green, and got home.

I expect we had tea, with perhaps toast and some chocolate or ginger cake.

And I would have read a book, or the papers, if it was Sunday.

I V

I don't remember any other details now, you see, except that this happened.

The sun shone, we had our walk, and there were two beautiful Burmese cats.

A Gift

Returning from the car, I come late home
And hear you weeping through the closed front door
Before the key scrapes in the lock. In the dark
I see you sitting, half way up the stair,
Curled in a foetus-shape as though in a womb,
Wearing your dressing-gown, striped red and gold,
As if for a ceremony not to take place,
Dressed up for birth, and still not to be born.

There are no words to show how much I care.
I go downstairs, close the door in my brain
On what seems too terrible to let out
Though it rips inside me. And then outside
In the quiet garden, behind the house,
I hear another sound, a scraping by stealth.
Turning, I reach to let in what I can.
I bring you the soft new hedgehog in my hands.

In the Same Room

Rain falls. Trickling on the flat roof
Where we face towards the mountains. The lake

On the other side stretches calmly
In the darkness. And the sounds lovers make

As they go to bed together filter in
From the corridor. You lie and read

And I lie and read in the same room
With my back to you. Whatever we need

From each other still, it isn't sex,
Or not that exactly. Creaking of beds

Rarely took place in our world. I speak
Now, and we both turn our tired heads

And you say, sweetly and softly, goodnight.
And the rain goes on falling. And that feels right.

Breaking Up

It begins to slide. In the wake of the sun,
Soft as tar,
They feel its edges grow viscous. As if spun

Just too far
Towards their heat, it sucks back, seethes. Only now
It is too late. Gradually, a long spar,

Like an axe, shapes itself on one side. Where their plough
Creaks, trembles at the brink, it opens, reveals
Fissures. How

They both react to that understanding seals
Its first gash
In ripples. You might have thought scraping of wheels,

Or a flash,
Would have warned them before. It seems not. These two
Were too close. In the orbit of their slow crash

Its glister formed a narrowing echo. Through
Plains of white
Veils, acres of their tears froze. Folded, snow flew

On a flat circle, receding through twilight
In complete dulled thunder, so that neither heard
Ice-turn, bite

Of toothed hail, or a frost-manacle. All furred
Thoughts were toys
In the warmth of a knowing touch. If each word,

Shape, employs
An edge on them now, that was earned. So they glide
Together in a sort of code, a grave poise

As of corners wrongly skated. If a hide,
A fleece, were stretched, scented with pole-wind, that one,
Hung inside,

Would shake, shiver. This one, glassed like a flare-gun
Which can fire
Only in caves of ice, would wince. In the sun,

Then, they stand, but are split now. Their stiff beech-pyre
Is the cause
Of those incisions, that flowing. A wet spire

Of glass, floors
Of slip-ice, trouble its grip. It nudges bare
Outlets. They watch it crumble, turn as it soars,

Almost without crust, for a nook in the air
To be at ease in. As with a cooling star,
It must share,

In the gravity of its fall, what they are
Now, were before,
And have renewed. It cracks to a wound, a scar.

A Driving Lesson

I lie in the slung bucket seat
With my hands on the wooden wheel. Through the windscreen
I see the buttered facades of the park. *You must press*
Your foot on the clutch in this car
Before you do anything else. Try. And she leans
Across me, her light hand on my knee.
We kiss between gears.

Outside the long rain slants
On the wound glass. The lesson continues.
Look. The accelerator is there
Beside your right foot. You must learn
To press it slowly. In this car
You could soon be in trouble.
Make sure the hand-brake is on.

The gears are in neutral. I put
The car into first, into second. We sit
Without moving. *In this car*
There is nothing to do in London. It ruins
The engine to cruise under forty. You see
You can't get to fourth. We hold hands,
Her hand with its ring in my hand.

There is nothing to do in London. We kiss
In the park. Outside in the violent world
There is rain. In this beautiful car
I am learning to drive, we lie in our separate
Seats, and I touch her arms
With the tips of my fingers, across the gears,
Watching the tears in her eyes.

A Divorce Poem

I

    That wooden sword I dreamed
    Several nights ago
Was the one my father made
    And wrapped in sticky tape
With vermilion paint on the blade

    For blood. In my dream it was yours,
    The one you gripped in a fight
Against someone twice your size
    You had to beat for your life
And who got you between the eyes.

    It was white and smooth, I remember,
    Curved like a scimitar
And with, somewhere, an awkward notch
    Like a bite out of a cake
Or the V in a woman's crotch.

I I

    Was that why? I wonder
    As I try to interpret the dream
Just why it sank, and then died,
    And then rose again the next night.
I suppose it may have implied

    That this patriarchal sword
    Was a weapon I much admired
When, in fact, it had lain unused
    In a cupboard of soldiers and toys.
Years later, I grew confused.

With my forefinger and thumb
I would stroke the line of the tape
And the vague edge of the splash
Where the paint suggested blood
With a scatter of drops like a rash.

But I feel a black hilt in my hand
And a curved blade enter my groin
As I write, and I dream again
When you lay your glasses aside
That I strike with the strength of ten.

The Truth

I

He listened, and could hear the light,
And that was what he came to hear:

The slow, long, trickling whiteness, and
The patches that were hard and clear.

At first, it had seemed far away,
And faint, and now it seemed too near.

II

He stared at it, until it grew,
And changed, and huge, strange faces came,

And watched him staring. Through the light
That settled on their skin, the same

Blue eyes he stared with stared at his,
As if they knew him, and his name.

III

But these blue eyes were like the sky
That he could see through covering glass.

He entered them for ever, and
There seemed no room for him to pass.

He turned his eyes, and saw the huge
Strange faces turn, and turn to glass.

IV

There seemed no time. There was no time
To understand why they had come,

And had to go so soon. He felt
A crudeness that was like a crumb

Along his eye, and then he breathed,
As if his body was a drum.

V

It seemed so to the watchers. They
Had settled into shapes of stone,

As beautiful as hers was now,
But empty, like a crib of bone.

Their serious expressions asked
For something gentle they could loan.

V I

And at that hour, across the world,
A man stepped in a cool cascade,

Naked, and swam. And nothing there
Was any help, or any aid.

Nothing he did, or said, that day.
Nothing he had, or loved, or made.

V I I

Happiness is a state of mind,
And grief is something frail and small.

I tell you this of grief. It dies,
And, when it dies, it hears the call

Of what lives on, and answers it,
With all its strength, once and for all.

Two Days After

When we lay down, I touched
Your breasts, and they were wet
With something white.
   I asked you, and you clutched
   Your silk shirt tight.
It brushed me. And I let

   Your hand stray down, and pluck
   At the blood below my jeans.
Your eyes were bold.
   You wanted me to fuck,
   And I was cold.
It seemed the future's means

   Lay in that darkening stain
   Where everything had stuck.
Your eyes grew mild.
   You beckoned me to suck
   Milk for our child
While death was still in flood.

   That night, as if in prayer,
   I entered you behind
With, I suppose, some pride
   In having you so bare
   Of what was in your mind,
Or what had grown inside.

   This lay now far away
   Unfettered, and untried,
And, perhaps, at rest.
   I came. And then I cried.
   And that seemed best,
I thought I heard you say.

An Hour Ago

I looked in the empty window
Where your easel stood in shadow
And the broom leaned in the corner
As I left it, after sweeping,
When we cleared away your paintings, and you packed them in
    the car.

I stood there in the twilight
And I felt the surge of darkness
As it flooded from the rafters
And came down to touch your door
In the softening of the moonlight, and the cooling of the day.

I remembered how the saddle
Hung along the whitewashed wall, and
The black outlines of your drawings,
And the blurred shapes gathering volume
As you worked there in the sunlight, with a book beside your
    hand.

I remembered how the thunder
Broke one day when we were talking
And we rose and watched sky blacken
In the courtyard, and the rain
Came and slanted down your window, and we lay and watched
    it slide.

I stood, and darkness thickened
As it drifted from the zenith,
And I felt the cold of night seep
Through the thinness of my shirt
As I turned away in silence, and the moon shone round and full.

I came in to this bare table
By my window, where the noise
Of late traffic from the freeway
Shook the balance of my mind,
And I felt your image tremble, and I moved to hold it still.

The Place of Being

I

It had fallen in, or been broken.
The top was in angles of slabs
   That lay sideways, slightly askew.
I could see the bare earth underneath.

The metal holder for flowers
Had gone. But a small green moss
   Was growing in earth in the casing.
I touched it with my thumb.

On the scatter of chips of granite
Some little plant was blooming
   That might have been heather. The headstone
Was stained, darkened with soot.

I I

It was cold in the wind on the hill,
But the view was quite beautiful.
   New buildings rose in the mist
In the valley, towers of concrete.

Somewhere down there, live people
Went about their autumn business,
   Forgetful of the dead in their graves.
As I had been, until now.

I stood for a moment with head bowed,
Wondering what to say.
   But I couldn't think of anything.
And it seemed stupid to kneel.

So I lifted a sycamore leaf
From the shallow drift on your bodies,
   And folded it into my pocket.
And then I walked away.

A Poem for Breathing

Trudging through drifts along the hedge, we
Probe at the flecked, white essence with sticks. Across
    The hill field, mushroom-brown in
    The sun, the mass of the sheep trundle
As though on small wheels. With a jerk, the farmer

Speaks, quietly pleased. *Here's one.* And we
Hunch round while he digs. Dry snow flies like castor
    Sugar from the jabbing edge
    Of the spade. The head rubs clear first, a
Yellow cone with eyes. The farmer leans, panting,

On the haft. *Will you grab him from the
Front?* I reach down, grope for greasy fur, rough, neat
    Ears. I grip at shoulders, while
    He heaves at the coarse, hairy
Backside. With a clumsy lug, it's up, scrambling

For a hold on the white, soft grass. It
Stares round, astonished to be alive. Then it
    Runs, like a rug on legs, to
    Join the shy others. Ten dark little
Pellets of dung steam in the hole, where it lay

Dumped, and sank in. *You have to probe with
The pole along the line of the rest of the
    Hedge. They tend to be close.* We
Probe, floundering in Wellingtons, breath
Rasping hard in the cold. The released one is

All right. He has found his pen in the
Sun. I dig in the spade's thin haft, close to barbed
    Wire. Someone else speaks. *Here's*
    Another. And it starts again. The
Rush to see, the leaning sense of hush, and the

Snow-flutter as we grasp for the quick
Life buried in the ivory ground. *There were*
    Ninety eight, and I counted
  Ninety five. That means one more. And I
Kneel to my spade, feeling the chill seep through my

   Boots. The sun burns dark. I imagine
The cold-worn ears, the legs bunched in the foetus
    Position for warmth. I smell
  The feathery, stale white duvet, the
Hot air from the nostrils, burning upwards. And

   I crouch above the sheep, hunched in its
Briar bunk below the hedge. From the field, it
    Hears the bleat of its friends, their
  Far joy. It feels only the cushions
Of frost on its frozen back. I breathe, slowly,

   Trying to melt that hard-packed snow. I
Breathe, melting a little snow with my breath. If
    Everyone in the whole
  World would breathe here, it might help. Breathe
Here a little, as you read, it might still help.

Not Making Platelets

You lay beside your view,
Huge, white, and bruised.
Above your arm, the drip
Oozed out a stain, where blood
    Moved down to make you new.

Time only would tell why.
Meanwhile, you lay and gazed.
The Thames ran slowly by.
Christmas had gone the way
    Only it can. And I,

Who visited you, saw
The agony behind
Your play of being glad
To be away from work.
    Your illness was a law

You had to obey. You turned,
Face grey with pain, and old,
As it never seemed before.
I felt tears come. I touched
    Your fever where it burned.

You were too ill to care
That I might be your heir
Through the tender line of kin.
Later, I might. For now,
    We spoke of what was there,

The drip above your bed,
The chart beside your arm,
And the quality of their food.
I admired the way you had piled
    The hair up on your head.

It seemed too strange a thought
That you could soon be dead.
Your blood refused to clot.
You smiled at me. You thanked me
   For the red flowers I'd brought.

I turned away in pain,
Thinking of others who
Had lain for me in bed,
My mother, Mr. Stokes.
   I turned to you again,

Examining each mark.
You were too far from blood
For a kiss. But there was this.
I touched you on the hand
   While rain fell through the dark.

The Creed

I

One day, perhaps, I shall die
In some foreign guerrilla war.
That's what it all seems for,
I think, sometimes, in my dreams.
I use the word dreams for hopes,
Or fears, or for my ideals,
Not for what happens in bed.
One day I shall be out there dead,
One mote in the terrible fire,
As if I had never been.
I have no fear of that.
I shall blink in the eye of the cat
The Egyptians thought the sun was.
Bravery comes in the night,
I suppose, the three o'clock kind,
When you wake, half-drunk, as I have,
Rising for water, or juice,
With your head in a dizzy whirl,
And thinking about your girl.
Well, the long night has its use
When it forces me into this
In lieu of sex, or a kiss.

I I

Alive still at forty six,
What do I care about?
I don't know, I really don't know.
But I feel what I feel, I know that.
Nobody can take away
Those creatures that watch in fur
I give life to, who give me life,
The gods, and toys, of my brain.
If they circle, they always return
To keep me safe while I sleep.
You can laugh, laugh if you dare.

Nothing matters but faith
To what matters inside the heart.
Write that down for a start.
I believe in the stress of the world,
In the insurgency of pain
That will go, and will come again.
We are under perpetual siege
By the powers of darkness. Yes,
And I'd have it no other way,
Child of that sluggish war,
As I am, that will never die.
There will always be bombers there
At the back of my burning head,
And my father in uniform.
I have no time for progress, or luck.
Sometimes it seems as if
I hunt at each party with claws,
I reach out for love with my teeth.
I go up when I hear the alarm,
Scrambled in fur in the cold.
With the dawn air on my chin,
They come into my sights at speed
And my body moves out to kill.
The enemy. No, the friends
I have to have or I die.

I I I

I feel colder now as I write,
And the alarm clock ticks up towards five.
Outside through the sash I can see
The light blue-green of the day.
I want to address this to you.
I need your name, at the end,
To make sense of the bitterness,
The rage, and the words in place.
You give me the force to write

As directly and flat as I've done.
I take energy out of your face
With my eyes. Off your skin
With my hands. Through your blood
By the penetration of love.
It needn't always be you.
I know, and I fear it won't.
It wasn't before, and I felt
The same as I do tonight.
But it's you today. And I feel
The intensity of it break
Into simple, clear-cut thoughts.
We think the same. You believe
In what I believe, a bit.
More than others do, you trust
In the myth of being brave.
I love you for that. And I will,
Even if things go wrong.
At least, I hope that I will,
And I hope that they won't tonight.
You're asleep with another man.
I trust you, and why you are,
And I trust you in loving me.
Trust here, perhaps, is hope.
I suppose only that. And yet
What else is there now, as I end,
With the blue-green growing grey,
And the sour taste of your drink
In my throat, and the need to sleep
Long gone, and another day
Out there to live in and deal with,
And three more until we meet?

In My Carriage From Redcar, I Felt Sad

But near Darlington, as the train
Slowed and came in, I saw a bedraggled bird
In my head, or it might have been on a concrete fence.
It was ruffling its feathers in the invisible wind
    Of some word
   Saying there might be a time for the pain
Of the earth-dragging to grow less intense
In the furrowing wake of knowing one might have sinned.
  I listened. And I, too, felt furred

    For a trip in the clearer air
Of being disentangled. I took my coat
From the rack, lugged up my pair of well-thumbed bags,
And was down on the platform. It seemed far less cold
    Out there
   Than when I had started. What smote
Me on the face was a warm breeze. The slag's
Loved odour slackened. I was not too old
  To scent the breath of something rare.

And I Bequeath

I

And I bequeath my sunflushed house
At Metton to the oak and pine.
May acorns fall with cones to line
Soft highways for the wandering mouse

When I am gone. For their slow fall
Throughout sweet autumn into snow
Was always welcome long ago
When I was there. And as for all

Such coarse developments of stone
As may repair, and spoil, their sway
I will them, by this hand, away.
But may they let nice care alone

For what I leave, those labouring arms
That may decide to halt loose weed
And save my lapsed estate from seed.
May these enjoy their shading charms.

I I

And I bequeath, near Holland Park,
My suite of rooms in pastel brown
To any man of means in town.
There let him blaze away the dark

With paper lanterns. For there I
Allowed the growth of paper space
And let my books assume the place
That others would have granted sky.

Such balustrades will long outlast
The sediments of Cantwell grime
And later prove, as in their prime,
A standing glory from the past.

And so let men look out along
My curving crescents, and admire
Their symmetry of crock and spire,
And quiz the daily passing throng.

III

And I bequeath my printed word
To men of honour in my trade
Who may tell what was carved and made
From what was merely glimpsed, or heard.

And may they publish, as they can,
Such decent parts by private sale
As may invite some praise, nor fail
To end the course that I began.

Otherwise, may all warp and fox
In volume or in open file
And finally, for lack of style,
Go blazing down from some old box.

And let the ashes, thinned from smoke,
Sift into London soil, and seem
To beckon flowers from their dream,
To blossom over polished oak.

IV

And I bequeath the folded claws
Of all my swords to those dead few
Who fought with grace against the new
In loyalty to formal laws.

May some caretaker gently wipe
All specks of dust from their drawn blades
And cherish them, by thoughtful aids
In secret, till the time be ripe

For conscious ownership to face
The enormous majesty of art,
And touch its tempered steel, and start
The resurrection of a race.

Then may their scabbards, delicate
With copper and the shine of gold,
Appreciated as of old,
Shimmer on stands, and glow in state.

V

And I bequeath my father's tools
In their bent box, his dressing-gown,
And what he took for work in town,
His compasses, to simple fools,

As I have been. For when he died
And left me what I touch and hold
The dour world was already old
In other ways. And I have tried

And failed so often to control
My gathered weight of grief and guilt
For what he might have loved, and built,
That I have shrivelled in my soul.

So let alone that envelope
With what he carried when he fell,
Before a place of flowers, tell,
And may the future know, my hope.

V I

And I bequeath what I know best,
My feelings, and I know them well,
To whatever shelters things in flow
And stores them in a proper chest.

And if they seem, like other cloth
Before the ravages of hate,
Mere things of dirt, of little weight,
Then lease them to the common moth.

There may they moulder where they rayed
In the bare heart of her I held
Whose narrow figure, once beheld,
I never fathomed, nor betrayed.

But let her sleeping head, some day,
Along the pillows of the grave
Lie smooth, and may some architrave
Of noble marble mark her sway.

VII

And I bequeath my empty head,
My hollow flesh, and leaking bones,
To those well nourished upon groans
Who operate upon the dead.

If any organ seem alive
And able to contain some spark
From what was formerly its dark
And lonely region, let them strive

And, if they will, transfer it whole
To some other spirit racked in pain
And needing help. And, if no gain
Be found in that, then let the mole

From Metton, whom I love and aid,
Accept the remnants, bleached in fire,
As compost for his common mire,
And thus my rent to life be paid.

The Celebration

I try to write
On foreign pine
With graphite, what I dreamed tonight.

I saw this man
We both admire:
Whose house we fill with our desire:

Whose head, like mine,
Was hot with fire:
Who died in nineteen twenty nine.

He was one part
Of that wide flame
That always burns and stays the same.

It sways us now,
And will again.
He shot his dear one through the brain

Five floors above.
Where we now kiss.
And there are miracles like this:

Where Josephine
And Harry died,
Your dark skin moves, like moving grain.

I celebrated
In my pride
His blazing strangeness. And you cried

Out as you came
In that same flame.
And it can never be denied.

The Flanders House

Whether I woke
Inside it, or was there before,
Or always, I could never tell:
Or whether what was shining broke
    Some spell,
And let through light. I used to knee the floor,

Hoping it might
Sink under me, and show my hall
Safe, as it used to be, my comb
Fixed in a brush to fit my height,
    My home
With all its warmth. Why paintings on a wall

Should hurt so much
I never knew, nor whence those came,
Nor what they showed. I saw, in oil,
The same blank faces wallow, touch,
    And spoil,
As I had seen in mud. Some trick, or game,

Was being played
On how I thought, or what I knew,
Before I could remember. Tiles
Notched in the ground made patterns, rayed
    In files,
That seemed in order. And a feeling grew

Of being turned
Inside a jar, or like a card,
To cue some echo. Far away,
A sense of something being burned
    In hay,
And crumbling, formed. What shifted, and was hard,

Near to the bed,
Or underneath my body, eased
And seemed more even then. I heard
A vice creak, and a voice that shed
Some word,
Or sound, shuffling the air. I touched, then seized

And gripped, the rod
Or barrel, of a wheel, or gun,
And felt a chill rise. Was it ice,
Or only metal of a hod,
Or one
Of those tarred flagstone rings? A taste of rice,

Crisp, wry, by rote,
Or was it oats, or could a horse,
If I had one, or was one, know
The two apart, rose, and my throat
Felt coarse
And raw. This all befell me long ago,

Or will occur
Some night soon, if I live to smell
The burning flesh, or grass, again,
And feel, through drifting smoke, the fur
On men
And dogs, and sleep in earshot of a shell.

The Saddled Man

All day you worked in the brick room, out
    Of the sun, under the pines,
Near to the stables. White violets rose through
    A bed of dry needles on
    The path curving to the bare grave. But

When it was dark, the dream came. In your
    Head, under the eaves, a slow
Whinnying started. Over the sloughed hands of
    Hemlock, a blundering of
    Muffled hooves. Uneasy, you walked to

The window. One June, in a spruce wood.
    You had drawn your breasts, naked
In a mirror, feeling the wind stir warm hair
    On your neck. Walking to church
    As a child, you had watched a mounted

Man bounce to a fox-hunt. Sun rang on
    The cold blood of his cap. Light
Galloped like a stallion behind your eyes, the
    Holy engine of noon. You
    Woke with the taste of stale hay on your

Tongue. Alert, you listened. Forming the
    Solid, moving smells in the
Dark stall. Touching the clink of stirrups, and the
    Heavy snaffle of warm breath.
    Exhausted, you slept. Accepting in

The womb of your nightmare that rider
    Drawn from the ashes of stilled
Flame. Charcoaled, with a saddle over his brain.
    Rising at the cock's crow, you
    Walked through the early sun to the grave's

Edge. In the light, falling now softly
Over your fondled cones, you
Stood waiting, anointing yourself with resin
At knee and shoulder. Far back
In the spruce wood, a horse was neighing.

A Poem of Death

FROM THE RUMANIAN OF MARIA BANUS

And once again the angel of Death came,
this time in the guise of a baker.
He had the clothes, the face, the hands of a baker,
and all of them white with flour.
In his hand he held a shovel,
from his ovens there came the smell
of bread burned in the fire.
His movements were solemn and stately.
The wheel, the blaze and the round bread
followed each other
slowly, and for ever,
from the mouth of the furnace.

I am not afraid of you, bread-maker,
you remind me of Janus,
in the street of childhood,
the paradise of cracknel.

This was my word to him
when he raised his hidden skull towards me.
Behind him the mills of Auschwitz were grinding
and the citizen bread-maker
in his apron powdered with flour,
angel of Death, angel of fire,
spread out before my eyes
his naked wares:
hollow they all were,
covered with mushrooms
close to the roots.

A Fear

I waited for you all the time,
    but you never came.
I don't think you ever had such
    a firm shape before.
Or perhaps it was just that I
    only realised it that day under the bed,
waiting for you to crawl out,
    and remembering your pipe-cleaner legs
in the poem Merle Kobatake
    wrote about you
in the toe of her shoe.

I watched on the concrete pavement
    outside my flat in Waikiki.
I listened to the story of how
    you once crouched
on a man's back, in a kimono,
    up the valley in Manoa.
But you never came.
    I remember the book
with your picture in it
    the boys had in Kaneohe,
a bit dog-eared, and as if borrowed.

But it was you all right,
    there as in the film
when Sean Connery woke up
    naked from his bath with
you on his shoulder.
    It must be the shoulder
for me that the vulnerable place
    is in, where I feel
the prickly, gooseflesh horror
    and turn, anguished, striking,
finding you even bigger than I expected.

Death of a Ferrari

IN MEMORIAM 840 HYK

I

It was made for the manager of Crockford's,
    Driven in a Monte Carlo Rally,
Owned by a salesman, later, at Maranello's,
    A retired colonel, then me.

I couldn't afford that wastrel elegance.
    I could scarcely carry
The seven-foot, iron exhaust system
    When it cracked, and broke, in Leeds.

I loved its worn, greyed ivory leather,
    The petrol-blue of its hide.
It growled along at 104
    With its bad brakes, and its leaking seal.

I can hear now that-famous,
    Belly-flustering Ferrari roar
Bounced back off the wall of the underpass
    One night, in Picadilly. It was like the blitz.

All right. So the door was rusted,
    Smoke came out of the dashboard wires
The first time I drove it on the M4.
    Who cares? It was a major car.

I I

It didn't crash on the motorway,
    Or blow up at 150.
It didn't burn itself out down a cliff
    Taking a bend too fast, in Scotland.

It was ditched in a car-park
    On Willesden Green.
So under the Civic Amenities Act 1967
    Section No. 20

Removal and Disposal of Abandoned Vehicles
    The Transport and Cleansing Division
Of the London Borough of Brent
    Will sell it for scrap.

Some other owner is responsible,
    The next sucker in the line.
But I feel tonight a remote sense of guilt
    Mixed with a tinge of outrage

To think of the rationality of that great engine
    Ripped into shreds,
The camshaft smashed, the radial tires torn loose,
    And the little dancing horse stripped from the grill.

It had electric windows, in 1961.
    It had the original radio, with its aerial.
It could out-accelerate any car in Europe.
    They don't come off the floor like that any more.

A Memory of the Thirties

As they turn, circling above the hill,
I see three dark heads, one a girl's, lift
    In the slipstream, gloved hands raised in

Salute, or to throw something. I shift
    Into third, racing for the burned mill
        Where someone is waving. On my skin

    I feel the silk of your gold scarf spill
        In a cool rustling. Vapour trails thin
Above the larches, begin to drift

    Over the wheel, like smoke. As I still
The arms, entering the yard, a rift
        Seems to break in the cloudbank. They pin

Minute brooches in blue, as they sift
    Air into air, climbing. In a spin
One is falling back, comes for the kill.

It is hers. There is only one gift
    Possible, the small capsule of tin
You are running to pick up. I fill

    My lungs with a long breath, in the din
Of the twin propellers. As with thrift,
    You break the capsule, swallow the pill.

The Mist

As we left Mainz, it drew in
More and more of the free surfaces. At first,
    Only a spire on a hill,
Or a sharp village, would, quite slowly, begin
    To lose place, to drown in it. The worst
Areas were over dark, annulled trees, till

    We left Frankfurt. At more speed,
Air drained away, emptying the immense train
    Of all it could shape. A deep
Layer of eroded seething, like the feed
    Pump of a lost machine, left a stain,
A wool-blur, on the rock-face. As if asleep,

    Hurtling towards a new dream,
Each carriage, growing warmer, gathered its light
    Into a ball. We lost hold
On something that could have been time. From the stream
    Of what was dissolving foreign height
Outside the window, a single tear-drop rolled,

    Swelled to a singular grain,
Was ice. Touched, we were travelling in the clear sheet
    Of a pane of glass, alone
Beyond confines of privacy. As the brain
    Absorbed its internal banked-up heat,
We moved on our trip. In the world of white stone

    Fractured by the mist, no sun,
Solidified out of human need, split frost
    From the rocks. Life was all hard
For ever. Seeming to turn black, things poised, spun,
    Then fell away, broken. What was lost
By this fathered its own movement. In the yard

Of a passed farm, a greyed ox
Lay on its knees, a statue. Through the peeled wood
   On the bluff behind, a white
Royalty of arriving tramps, with a box
   Of mysterious green perfumes, could
Service, we were able to see, our god. Flight

   Of a train could never stay
Such advancing reluctances. The mist rose,
    As it came, revealing towers
In its gathered thinning. Somehow it made play
   With its own habits. As if it chose
To be a bride, the landscape unveiled skirts, flowers.

A Girl's Dream

You sent me to a school. You said they'd teach me
    How to love you there. O
Yes, I said, where is it? Tell me where it

Is. It was a big house. There were window
    Panes with thin bars. In the
Hall they met me with stiff aprons. Take your

Clothes off, come in here, they said. O yes, I
    Said, yes. Lie down here, they
Said, and put this army blanket on you.

Rub this oil on. Watch the others. It will
    Take time. Take it slowly.
So I lay down by the window. I could

See behind a screen. There was a girl there
    Who looked used to it. Then
Someone came and said that she was doing

Well. Look there, they said, she's torn a hole. That's
    Good. That's what we like. Try
Harder now. I had tried hard. I went on

Trying. All I felt was being by the
    Light, though. Someone might see.
Then you came. You looked down at me, didn't

Speak. And then you took your shirt off, then your
    Socks and shoes. And then you
Lay down on the bed beside me, kept your

String vest on. I couldn't just go on not
    Doing anything, though,
Could I? So I got up, ran out. Through the

Hall I ran and out the front door. No-one
   Stopped me. It was raining.
Look, I said, a church. All black with grime, it

Had a dome just like St. Paul's but smaller.
   When the clean rain hit my
Oiled flesh, I felt better. There were white steps.

I ran up them. No-one saw me. And the
   Cool rain washed my face and
Body till the oil was all washed off. And

I was up there on the white steps wearing
   Nothing all alone. And
It was all right. It was really all right.

For the Union Jack

Faffling now, as if at
     Some point of achieved vantage (the
Whole fire sucked through the staff into
          That flame) it

Afflicts the blunt wind, an abrupt
     Britannic intransigeance by
Fiat of (or would one perhaps be
          Exposed, conceding

Rather, in fief to)
     Some taloned excellence: nor
Flawed by, nor intolerant in,
          Too free a play of

Sick pride in the map bleeding
     Incontinence of an
Old bitch gone in the hilts (I
          Mean, England and

All that) it
     Ails, droops, drowned in the
Cataract of imagined (no, I
          Aver, *false*) courtesy and

Referred bloodshed: outriding
     The new embassies
A-flutter in what was before
          Their adjusted moment a, well,

Maid's cubby-hole: and yet still (and
     Not, no not purely
To be teasing luck out further) I note
          Alertly, yes, alertly

Over the fine hint of a suave
    Persistence in
Lobbying that old and no longer (surely) so
    Obvious patriot

Sunset, bellying out in (great-rooted, blossoming, and
    So criss-crossed with the
Swords of the dead managers you could
    Hardly mistake it for

Shell's, Ghana's or Selfridge's, or
    Not with that cool
Initiative to be lead-taking) the, well,
    Yes, one kind of, rain.

For the Arrival of a New Cat

The new cat is coming, is coming, the
green frog with glass eyes
    is croaking. He squats
  in the grate on his three legs in
    faience alertness. Beside him the
pot bear with
black eyes is lifting
  his nosed head, he
    sniffs at the temperature, and
is ready. Outside in

  the garden, the fuchsia is
ringing its red bells in
    Japanese pleasure. It
  dangles its tongues in delight. The
    spirea
flourishes plumage of pink which is
blue when
  you look at it closer. The new cat is
    coming, is coming, the
roses expect him. Upstairs, in

  the attic, the locked trunks are
creaking. Their papers and letters
    grip their teeth tightly. The
  new cat is coming, is coming, the
    books on their white shelves are
scattering leaves to receive him, their
spines are his servants. The
  carpet with purple pagodas is
    buffing its flat felt to
make him a warm bed. The new cat is

coming, he moves with his
cone tail
    into the passage-way, over the wall, and,
    with tumbling abandon,
        down along bumpy and moss-filled stones to
the house he will live in. He
opens
    his new mouth and silently,
        almost silently.
screams a small welcome. The

    storm which has gathered is breaking, the
hotness expands and
    explodes in a fanfare of
raining and thunder. Inside, by the window,
    the new cat is watching, is
watching. The new cat has come and
the storm is
    his celebration. With slit ears, he
    frowns through the glass which
is wet, and protects him. The

    new cat is coming, is coming, the weather
intones his arrival, it
    spells it with showers, and lightning
    flashes across four gardens to
    mix him a joy-song. He
turns on his back, and
rolls over and sleeps
    with his paw on his face. He is
    tired, the new cat
is tired, the new cat is sleeping.

    As he sleeps, he is dreaming, he
dreams of a rainbow. It
    burgeons, and flowers,

    fluttering petals of peonies, meat-red
        and pretty. The new cat
dives in his dream through a paradise
thick with the perfume
   of coley
      and raw steak. The new cat has
come to his house, he is happy.

The Day the World Ended

FOR JOHN BETJEMAN

The washing machine was whirling away,
    The cat was licking its tail,
A pile of clothes was on top and done,
    And a pile was below in a pail.

The basement was growing steamy and warm,
    The cat was alert and wise,
The dryer was doing its job quite well,
    And the jeans were rattling their flies.

The regular wash was all clean and dry,
    The *Tide* was back on the sink,
The handkerchiefs were all fresh and smooth,
    And the towels looked bright and pink.

The revolving drum had come to a halt,
    The shirts were all shut inside,
The air was thick with the smell of suds,
    And the cat's eyes were open wide.

The world was travelling round the sun,
    The moon was out in the West,
A spider was tottering over the floor,
    And the maid was wringing a vest.

The hangers were on the clothes horse,
    The socks were dripping and wet,
The cat had gone for a plate of fish,
    And the sun had started to set.

The light was up in the living-room,
    The lamp was down in the hall,
The cat was hunting a brown rat,
    And nothing had happened at all.

The Flame of Love, By Laura Stargleam

A MILLS AND BOON POEM

I

Garth Symbel strode up the hill towards
the dark bulk of Lornewood Castle, grimly
silhouetted against the setting sun. The harsh

contours of his swarthy face were set in dour
lines as he thought back over what had happened
in the shadow of the dripping laurels earlier that

winter afternoon. Lorelei Fairstance was
a mere chit of a girl, but the tilt of her
little nose and the jut of her pretty hips

had been too much for the pent-up feelings
of Garth's wicked neighbour, Aldrich
Mindslade.

I I

Garth gripped the horsewhip

tighter in his powerful fist as he burst through
the flanking bushes at the gates of the mansion. Yes,

the man was going to be taught a lesson he
would remember for a long while, Garth was sure
of that. "Garth!" Lorelei was waiting

beside the old oak outside the narrow
Gothic windows of the conservatory. In the gathering
twilight, the moon shone lightly on the

waterfall of chestnut hair that fell over
her delicate shoulders, now partly exposed under
the straps of her Dior evening dress.

III

"Lorelei!"

Garth spoke with a touch of surprise. He
had not expected to meet his future bride
here before he had taught the would-be usurper

a lesson. "I hadn't expected to see you out
so late. You'll catch your death of cold in
that light wrap. Here, let me cover

you up." Lorelei moved away, drawing in her
breath with a touch of suppressed excitement to
feel his boldly male hand reach out for

the bare skin of her shoulder. "Garth. No." she
whispered. "Not now." She drew the shawl
tighter over herself, shrinking back against

the warm stone of the old castle wall.

I V

"Why,
Lorelei. You silly little girl. I'm not going
to hurt you. I worship the very ground you

tread upon. You know that. I'm here to
teach that scoundrel Aldrich Mindslade he can't
play around with your affections." Lorelei

put her hand to her mouth. A little gasp
came out, as she heard Garth speak these fateful
words.

V

"O Garth. No." she said. "He

meant no harm. I promise you that. I
wonder if it wasn't half my own fault." Garth
laughed shortly. "Well, in that wisp of an

evening dress, I can understand how
you might think that." he said. "But the
man must be taught to control his passions. I

mean to give him a taste of this." And
he cracked the horsewhip in the cool air

V I

Lorelei
gave out a little cry. "Garth. Garth," she

whispered. "Let him be. I beseech you.
No harm has been done yet by his folly, but
if you flog him now there will be

lasting feud between our houses." Garth Symbel
frowned. He looked up at the castle towering away
to the moon. "May be," he said. "But it can't

be helped."

V I I

At this moment the slim figure of Aldrich
Mindslade appeared round the corner of the house. Lorelei
screamed. It was going to be a bitter

confrontation. "Mindslade," said Garth. "I
was looking for you. I'm going to teach you a
lesson you won't forget. Stand over there

by that old tree.

VIII

"Symbel," said Aldrich
Mindslade. "I know what you're thinking. But
please don't judge me too harshly. I

love Lorelei and I mean to marry her. If
I was carried away today in the heat of passion,
I'm sorry. She knows that." A dark

wave of anger swept across Garth Symbel's
handsome face, and his fingers clenched on
the stem of the whip. "Marry her," he

ground out. "Why, you swine. You aren't fit
to sweep the grass she walks on. She's mine.
And never you forget it."

IX

"Garth, O Garth."

Lorelei rushed forward and flung herself
madly into Garth Symbel's arms. "I never
thought you cared. Why did you never say?

O Garth. Leave him alone, and kiss me.
Here. Now. In the garden. Do what you will!"
It was all that Garth could do to

hold in the rising tide of his passion. With
a curt gesture he motioned to Aldrich
Mindslade to leave them alone, and

the other man slunk off into the darkness.

X

By
the light of the moon Garth gazed down
    into Lorelei's fair head on his

    shoulder. He threw the whip aside. "My
dear sweet little girl," he said. "Not
    here. Not now. I want it to be so right

    the very first time with you. And that
means when we're married. In a church." The
    rush of feeling was almost more than

    Lorelei   could   stand.

X I

                    She felt her heart
pulsing under her thin straps. "O yes, Garth,
    yes," she found herself saying. And

    out beyond her in the sky the frail
moon seemed to sing like a bird as it
    sailed over the battlements. And in

    her heart joy spread its wings like a
dove and she knew that from now on
    everything, everywhere, was always going to be all right.

George MacBeth

George MacBeth was born in Scotland; he now divides his time between London and Norfolk. In addition to his books of poems he is the author of two books for children, *Noah's Journey* and *Jonah and The Lord;* a book of autobiographical prose pieces, *My Scotland,* and four novels, *The Transformation, The Samurai, The Survivor* and *The Seven Witches;* he is also the editor of several anthologies, the most recent of which was *The Book of Cats.*